Pebble®
Plus

How to Make a
Liquid Rainbow

Hands-On
SCIENCE
FUN

by Lori Shores

Consulting Editor: Gail Saunders-Smith, PhD

Consultant: Ronald Browne, PhD
Department of Elementary & Early Childhood Education
Minnesota State University, Mankato

CAPSTONE PRESS
a capstone imprint

Pebble Plus is published by Capstone Press,
151 Good Counsel Drive, P.O. Box 669, Mankato, Minnesota 56002.
www.capstonepub.com

 Books published by Capstone Press are manufactured with paper
containing at least 10 percent post-consumer waste.

Library of Congress Cataloging-in-Publication Data
Shores, Lori.
   How to make a liquid rainbow / by Lori Shores.
       p. cm.—(Pebble plus. Hands-on science fun)
   Includes bibliographical references and index.
   Summary: "Simple text and full-color photos instruct readers how to make a liquid rainbow and explain the science
behind the activity"—Provided by publisher.
   ISBN 978-1-4296-5294-0 (library binding)
   ISBN 978-1-4296-6216-1 (paperback)
   1. Rainbow—Experiments—Juvenile literature. 2. Science—Study and teaching (Preschool)—Activity programs—
Juvenile literature. I. Title. II. Series.
   QC976.R2S56 2011
   530.078—dc22
                                                                           2010024909

Editorial Credits
Erika L. Shores, editor; Gene Bentdahl, designer; Sarah Schuette, photo shoot direction; Marcy Morin, scheduler;
   Laura Manthe, production specialist

Photo Credits
All photos by Capstone Studio/Karon Dubke except page 5 (background), Shutterstock/irin-k

Note to Parents and Teachers

The Hands-On Science Fun series supports national science standards related to physical
science. This book describes and illustrates how to make a liquid rainbow. The images support
early readers in understanding the text. The repetition of words and phrases helps early readers
learn new words. This book also introduces early readers to subject-specific vocabulary words,
which are defined in the Glossary section. Early readers may need assistance to read some
words and to use the Table of Contents, Glossary, Read More, Internet Sites, and Index sections
of the book.

Printed in the United States of America in North Mankato, Minnesota.
092010
005933CGS11

Table of Contents

Rainbow in a Jar 4

Making a Liquid Rainbow 6

How Does It Work? 16

Glossary 22

Read More 23

Internet Sites. 23

Index 24

Safety Note:
Please ask an adult for help when making a liquid rainbow.

Rainbow in a Jar

Rainbows reach across the sky.
You can build a liquid rainbow
in a jar.

Here's what you need:

½ cup (120 mL)
light corn syrup

½ cup (120 mL)
blue dish soap

½ cup (120 mL)
water

½ cup (120 mL)
olive oil

½ cup (120 mL)
rubbing alcohol

3 mugs

1-quart (1-liter) jar

spoon

red, blue, and green
food coloring

Making a Liquid Rainbow

Pour ½ cup corn syrup
into a mug.

Stir in 1 drop each of blue
and red food coloring.

Pour the purple corn syrup into a jar.

Next, slowly pour ½ cup blue dish soap into the jar.

Pour ½ cup water
into another mug.

Stir in 2 drops of
green food coloring.

Tilt the jar. Very slowly pour
the green water along
the inside of the jar.

Then, slowly pour ½ cup
olive oil into the jar.

In another mug, stir 2 drops
red food coloring into
½ cup rubbing alcohol.
Tilt the jar and very slowly
pour in the rubbing alcohol.

Stand back and take a look.
Do you see a rainbow?

How Does It Work?

Liquids are made up of very tiny particles. How tightly packed these particles are determines density. Dish soap floats on corn syrup because the soap is less dense.

You carefully poured the water

so it wouldn't mix with the soap.

Water is less dense than dish soap.

The water floated on top.

Not all liquids can mix.

The oil didn't mix with the water.

Did the rubbing alcohol mix

with the oil?

Which one was denser?

Glossary

density—how closely packed particles are in a liquid or in an object

liquid—a wet substance that can be poured

particle—a very small piece of something

tilt—to tip to one side

Read More

Mezzanotte, Jim. *Liquids.* States of Matter. Milwaukee: Weekly Reader Early Learning Library, 2007.

Royston, Angela. *Solids, Liquids, and Gases.* My World of Science. Chicago: Heinemann Library, 2008.

Williams, Zella. *Experiments with Solids, Liquids, and Gases.* Do-It-Yourself Science. New York: PowerKids Press, 2007.

Internet Sites

FactHound offers a safe, fun way to find Internet sites related to this book. All of the sites on FactHound have been researched by our staff.

Here's all you do:

Visit *www.facthound.com*

Type in this code: 9781429652940

Super-cool stuff! Check out projects, games and lots more at **www.capstonekids.com**

Index

corn syrup, 6, 8, 16

density, 16, 18, 20

dish soap, 8, 16, 18

floating, 16, 18

food coloring, 6, 10, 14

liquids, 4, 20

mixing, 18, 20

olive oil, 12, 20

particles, 16

rubbing alcohol, 14, 20

water, 10, 12, 18, 20

Word Count: 204

Grade: 1

Early-Intervention Level: 20